D0324413

This Book Belongs To

_____

ELVIS

Theresa Celsi

Ariel Books

Andrews and McMeel
Kansas City

Respectfully dedicated
to the memory of
Elvis Presley

"The effect I have on audiences mostly comes from simple rhythm. Rhythm is something you either have or don't have, but when you have it, you have it all over."

*G*raceland, the home of the late Elvis Presley, attracts more than six hundred thousand visitors each year. When it was built, it lay south of Memphis, but the city grew to engulf it. The fourteen-acre estate includes the mansion, a swimming pool, and a meditation garden with the graves of Elvis and his mother and father.

When Elvis was alive, Graceland was

his refuge. After his death, it was opened to the public as a memorial. Another memorial was opened in Tupelo, Mississippi, Elvis Presley's birthplace. Two life-sized statues of Elvis have been dedicated: one in 1978 in Las Vegas and the other in 1988 in Germany. In January 1993, on the anniversary of his birthday, the U.S. government issued a postage stamp in his honor. And more than fifteen years after his death, millions of fans still travel thousands of miles to see his home and still buy his recordings and collect his memorabilia.

Why all this fuss? Why are so many millions of people still fascinated by a rock singer? What is the power of Elvis Presley?

GROWING UP

Gladys Smith Presley was in her last month of pregnancy when the New Year's bells rang in 1935. Although she had no real way of knowing, she had been sure from the beginning of her pregnancy that she was carrying twin boys. In fact, she already had names for them: Elvis Aron and Jessie Garon.

Gladys was right—she delivered twins

on January 8. But the older one, Jessie, was stillborn. From that day on, Gladys doted on the surviving child, Elvis, with all the love she had been planning for two.

It was the depths of the Great Depression, and Gladys and her husband, Vernon, lived in Mississippi, one of the poorest states in the Union. Before she had become pregnant, Gladys had a good job as a garment worker. Now she and Vernon could not even afford the doctor's fee for the delivery.

They were hard times, and Vernon had to be away for much of his son's childhood for economic reasons. When Elvis was two, Vernon left for two years to work on a cotton plantation. During those times alone, Elvis and Gladys became very close. She couldn't bear for Elvis to be out of her sight and walked him to and from school each day, even when he was in high school. They were so close that they developed their own affectionate language.

The family attended church every Sunday, and when he was nine, Elvis was baptized. He started actively practicing his religion by giving away his comic books and toys. This generosity stayed with him all his life: As a child, he gave away his tricycle; as an adult, he gave away Cadillacs.

Elvis's first taste of fame came when he was eleven. One of his teachers persuaded him to enter the talent contest at the Mississippi-Alabama Fair and Dairy Show. Elvis sang "Old Shep," a song about a beloved pet dog that had died. He won second prize—five dollars.

Around that time, his parents bought him a guitar. Elvis had wanted a rifle, but his mother vetoed that—a guitar was much less dangerous. Although Elvis was upset about not getting the rifle, he learned some chords and taught himself to play.

In 1946, the Presleys moved into Tupelo proper, where over the next two years they lived in several poor neighborhoods. Here, Elvis met his first real-life musician, a singer named Mississippi Slim, who broadcast from a local radio station every Saturday in front of a small audience. Through a classmate who happened to be the singer's brother, Elvis got into the broadcasts and watched the performances with awe.

In 1948, when Elvis was thirteen, the family moved to Memphis, Tennessee, where he attended L. C. Humes High School. He was an ordinary, but painfully shy, student. Gladys didn't permit him to play out of her sight until he was fifteen. Like all teenagers, he experimented with different looks, finally settling on a bold, slick pompadour hairstyle. At the time it seemed odd because most of the other boys wore crewcuts, so Elvis felt different and lonely.

In his senior year, Elvis began playing his guitar and singing for his fellow stu-

dents. After hearing him play at a home-room picnic, his teacher asked him to be in the annual variety show. Elvis sang "Old Shep" again. The other students loved his singing and went wild, but he could hardly believe it. "They really like me!" he kept saying to his teacher. For the shy young Elvis, that moment signaled a turning point. No longer would he be the lonely kid with a weird haircut. Because of his music, he was accepted.

SUN RECORDS

In the summer of 1953, eighteen-year-old Elvis was a truck driver for an electric company. On July 18, he walked into the Memphis Recording Service, which was offering a special. Anyone could come in and record a song for four dollars. Elvis recorded "My Happiness" and "When Your Heartaches Begin" as a birthday gift for his mother. The studio's office manager, Marion Keisker, didn't usually pay much attention to the people who came in. But there was something different about this

19

singer, something special, something sexy. She saved the tapes from the recording to play for her boss, Sam Phillips.

Phillips was impressed. He had been recording several black singers and selling the tapes to a record company in Chicago. But white stations wouldn't play the music, so Phillips couldn't get enough exposure to really sell the records. He decided that if he found a white singer who could sing like a black singer, he could sell records. Listening to Elvis's tapes, he knew he had found what he was looking for.

The next year, Elvis returned to the studio to make another birthday record. This time, Sam Phillips was there and asked Elvis for his phone number. He told the young man that he might have some work for him in a few months.

True to his word, Phillips asked Elvis to record at the studio that summer, teaming him up with Bill Black and Scotty Moore. After a few false starts, they recorded two songs, "That's All Right, Mama" and an uptempo version of "Blue Moon of Kentucky." These were released under the label of Sun Records.

Phillips took the record to a local radio station. As soon as it went on the air, the station switchboard lit up with people calling in to ask about the record. Quickly, Phillips got Elvis to the studio for an impromptu interview.

The record became a local hit. Elvis and his backup musicians started playing area places. Phillips's success with Elvis began attracting more young white singers to the studio. Soon, he had signed not only Elvis, but also Johnny Cash, Carl Perkins, and Jerry Lee Lewis. He called these four singers his "million-dollar quartet."

People loved Elvis's records, but his live performances drove them crazy. His sexually insinuating undulations excited the crowd into a frenzy. Some female fans actually passed out from hysterics. By the end of the year, Elvis not only was a popular live singer, but also was singing weekly on a radio show called "Louisiana Hayride" for the grand salary of eighteen dollars per show. When the show was televised, Elvis decided that he could make a living singing and quit his job driving trucks. Soon after, Elvis met the man who would make him a superstar: Colonel Tom Parker.

COLONEL TOM PARKER

Colonel Tom Parker was born Andreas Cornelius van Kujik in Breda, Holland. When he was eighteen, he came to the United States, entering the country illegally by jumping ship in New Jersey. After serving in the U.S. Army, he went into show business. He served as an advance man for country entertainer Minnie Pearl and for the Grand Ole Opry, then went on to manage country stars Eddie Arnold and Hank Snow.

When Parker met Elvis, he tossed the

others aside. Although Elvis already had a contract with disc jockey Bob Neal, Neal realized that the singer would be better off with Parker. When Neal let his contract with Elvis expire, Elvis signed with Parker.

The first thing the Colonel did was get Elvis a contract with another recording studio. Elvis would need a bigger label than Sun Records for nationwide distribution. Parker persuaded RCA to buy out Elvis's contract with Sun.

Sam Phillips wasn't happy to see Elvis leave, but he figured that the thirty-five thousand dollars he got from RCA would help him promote the rest of the million-dollar quartet. In one way, it was a good decision. The remaining members of the quartet—Johnny Cash, Carl Perkins, and Jerry Lee Lewis—did go on to become legends in their own right. But none of them ever touched Elvis in reputation or income. Phillips lost out on millions.

On the other hand, Elvis might never have become what he did without Colonel Tom Parker. Parker spent all his time promoting Elvis. Besides getting the singer a five-thousand-dollar bonus to sign with

"Rock and roll has been around for many years. It used to be called rhythm and blues.... I don't think it'll ever die completely out because they're gonna have to get something mighty good to take its place."

E L V I S

RCA, Parker was able to get fifty thousand dollars for three appearances on the "Ed Sullivan Show" and two film contracts, one with Paramount and one with MGM. Elvis was guaranteed one hundred thousand dollars for each film (he made up to three a year), plus a share of the profits.

People around the country reacted the same way the local folks had when they saw Elvis perform. They flipped for the young singer with the snarling lip and the swiveling hips. Young women screamed and seemed to go insane, sometimes rioting and tearing off Elvis's clothes. Elvis was nicknamed "Elvis the

E L V I S

Pelvis." He didn't like this name, calling it "a childish expression."

The hysteria disturbed a lot of older people, who couldn't understand what Elvis was doing and didn't like it. Even Frank Sinatra, who had made plenty of women swoon, thought Elvis was vulgar.

At first, Ed Sullivan refused to have Elvis on his popular TV variety show at all. When he finally did, the young women in the audience became almost uncontrollable when the sexy performer started moving. For many TV viewers, it was the first time they had ever seen this kind of performance. They were shocked!

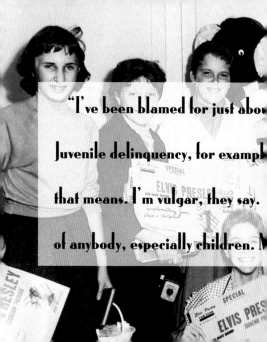

"I've been blamed for just abou

Juvenile delinquency, for exampl

that means. I'm vulgar, they say.

of anybody, especially children. M

erything wrong in this country.

—that I give kids 'ideas,' whatever

uldn't do anything vulgar in front

lks didn't bring me up that way."

On subsequent shows, Sullivan ordered that Elvis be filmed only from the waist up.

The controversy was disturbing to Elvis. He had always tried to be a good boy. He went to church, worked hard, and was respectful of his parents. Now he was being called vulgar and obscene.

FAME AND FORTUNE

Within two years, Elvis went from being a forty-dollar-a-week truck driver to having more money than he could count. In fact,

before he had met the Colonel, Elvis had never been inside a bank.

Elvis spread the good fortune around. He was known for buying cars by the dozens and giving them away as gifts. He hired several of his friends from high school and all of his relatives to take care of things—his money, his tours, and just keeping the fans from tearing him to pieces.

In 1957, he bought Graceland, a beautiful mansion on fourteen acres of land. Elvis had a kidney-shaped swimming pool built on the grounds, pillars added to the

"It's hard to explain rock and roll. It's a beat that gets you. You feel it."

front of the house, and a gate installed at the entrance to the estate to ensure his privacy. Inside, he put in two soda fountains, a jukebox, and a golden piano. His parents planted a vegetable garden and built a chicken coop in back of the house. Over the years, Graceland underwent many renovations as Elvis's tastes changed. At various times the interior was decorated in Elvis's favorite colors.

When Elvis bought Graceland, he was at the top of the world with a bright future. He

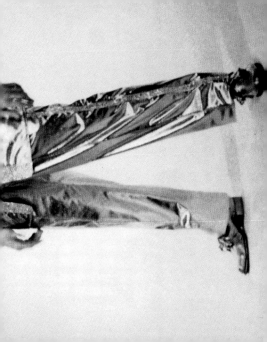

was known as the King of Rock and Roll. He had already made seventeen gold records. He was seeing a beautiful woman named Anita Wood. He was traveling all over the country, giving concerts and making movies. It seemed like nothing could stop Elvis. Nothing but the government, that is.

UNCLE SAM WANTS YOU, ELVIS

On December 10, 1957, Elvis received his draft notice from the U.S. Army. Since he was scheduled to film *King Creole*, he was

allowed to wait until March 1958 to enter the army. Although his fans protested, Elvis willingly put on the uniform, kissed Anita goodbye, and even sacrificed his famous hairstyle for a regulation crewcut.

Elvis was willing to serve his country, but he hated the thought of breaking up his friends and family. He arranged to have his entire entourage follow him, first to boot camp in Texas, and then to Germany, where he was stationed.

While Elvis was still in boot camp, Gladys fell ill. She was so sick that she and

Vernon returned to Memphis so she could enter a hospital. By August, her condition had become so grave that Elvis was granted a weekend pass to visit her. He stayed for thirty-six hours, until she begged him to get some rest. While he was asleep, she died.

Elvis was heartbroken. He and his mother had been closer than most mothers and sons. Gladys had been very opposed to Elvis's induction, terrified that he would be killed. Although she had had health problems before Elvis was drafted, that stress undoubtedly had contributed to her condition. Even with all his friends and family following him to Germany to keep him company, Elvis went overseas with a very heavy heart.

PRISCILLA

While Elvis was in the army, he met the great love of his life—his future wife, Priscilla Beaulieu. The daughter of a U.S. officer stationed in Germany, she came to a party Elvis threw in his private house, and for the entire evening he couldn't take his eyes off the beautiful young woman in the white sailor suit. By the time he returned to the United States, Elvis knew that he wanted to marry Priscilla.

Unfortunately, Priscilla was only fourteen—too young to get married. So Elvis made an arrangement with Priscilla's parents to let her come to Memphis to live with his family and attend a Catholic school. When she was twenty-one, she and Elvis would be married.

"I learned a lot about people in the army. I never lived with other people before and had a chance to find out how they think. It sure changed me, but I can't tell you offhand how."

A DIFFERENT KING

When Elvis returned to the United States, he was different. Maybe it was because of being in the army, or the death of his mother, or meeting Priscilla, or a combination of these. But he was less of a rebel and more mature, more relaxed. He stopped gyrating as wildly as he had when he performed, and he sang more ballads. Indicative of his new style was one of his 1960 gold records, "It's Now or Never," a version of the classic Italian song "O Sole Mio." The song had

been recorded by Italian opera tenors Enrico Caruso and Mario Lanza.

Elvis's new, softer image did not lose him his loyal fans; perhaps they, too, were getting a little older. Instead, he gained new ones. Even Frank Sinatra appeared with Elvis onstage.

In 1966, Elvis stopped recording and giving concerts. Instead of spending his talent and energy developing his music, he just coasted. He often stayed up all night, throwing parties for himself and his friends.

Elvis's career was also suffering because

"I'm sort of getting tired of being Elvis Presley."

of the movies he made. Colonel Parker had not been interested in making quality films or in developing Elvis as an actor; he was interested in making as much money as possible from Elvis's celebrity. Although Elvis was an electric performer, the screenplays for his movies never utilized his talent. They all followed the same formula: Elvis meets girl, Elvis gets girl—with Elvis singing as many songs as possible in between. And their quality ranged from mediocre to downright awful. The films made money, but they did not bring out

Elvis's talents, and the soundtrack albums did not sell.

By the late 1960s, Elvis's career was in a serious decline. Something had to be done. His failure to do live performances, his bad movies, and his absence from the recording studio had not lost him old fans so much as kept him from attracting new ones. The teenagers had new acts to idolize: the Beatles, the Rolling Stones, the Doors. Although these groups idolized the singer, Elvis was an old man compared to them. When he recorded a gospel music album, he began to seem hopelessly mainstream to the public. The Colonel knew something had to be done to save Elvis's career.

THE COMEBACK

Elvis's personal life took a turn in May 1967 when he and Priscilla finally married. Nine months to the day after their wedding, Priscilla gave birth to their daughter, Lisa Marie.

In 1968, Colonel Parker arranged for Elvis to appear on television. Originally conceived as a Christmas special, the show became a return to the Elvis of old, before he had gotten "safe." Elvis appeared in a black leather outfit that created a whole new sexy image. He had lost weight, and his high black pompadour was back. He looked and sounded fantastic! The critics raved, and the fans went wild. Elvis was back!

Colonel Parker made sure that Elvis never disappeared again. He booked him into the giant showplaces of Las Vegas, a glittering gambling empire that suited the larger-than-life singer. Elvis adapted to Las

Vegas by wearing more and more spectacu-
lar outfits, such as gold lamé jumpsuits with
long capes.

As the song goes, the nightlife isn't always
the good life. It can be confining and, after a
performance, boring. Elvis often stayed up
until eight in the morning, sleeping until the
middle of the afternoon. His free time was
spent watching privately screened movies
or enjoying an amusement park.

Elvis's career was back on track, but his
personal life was in upheaval. Although
Elvis was a strong personality, Priscilla had

a good sense of herself. By 1972, she realized that she wasn't happy married to Elvis, so they were soon divorced. However, she and Elvis remained cordial and shared custody of Lisa Marie.

THE LAST YEARS

The last five years of Elvis's life were much the same as they had been since he had become a superstar. He was fabulously wealthy—and was still incredibly popular. He still made records and gave concerts.

E L V I S

One of his concerts was beamed from Hawaii all over the world. Another was attended by all four Beatles, who were thrilled to finally see onstage the man who had inspired them.

Unexpectedly, on August 16, 1977, Elvis collapsed at Graceland. He was rushed to the hospital, where doctors tried to revive him. But it was too late: The King was dead at only forty-two.

Twenty thousand fans mourned at his funeral, and afterward Elvis was laid to rest beside his beloved mother, Gladys. When

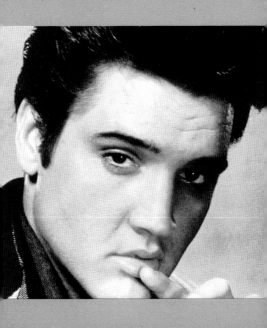

she had died in 1958, he had been uncontrollable in his grief, throwing himself on her coffin. Now he would be able to rest with her forever.

Within a month, someone tried to steal Elvis's body. Vernon had both Elvis's and Gladys's bodies moved from the cemetery to Graceland, where the security could be better maintained. They now rest in the meditation garden. When Vernon died in 1979, he was buried next to his wife and child. The family was reunited for eternity.

GONE BUT NOT FORGOTTEN

What has happened since Elvis's death is almost as fascinating as the story of his life. Many of his fans are so devoted that they find it hard to accept that Elvis has actually died. Absurd rumors have started that Elvis had faked his own death. Books have actually been written on the subject. Other fans believe that Elvis is in heaven, watching over and sending messages to his fans.

Still others want so much to see Elvis again that they settle for seeing Elvis re-creations. There are hundreds of Elvis impersonators who try to look and sing like the King. Even at the centennial celebration of the Statue of Liberty, the festivities included a tribute to Elvis featuring two hundred impersonators.

Hundreds of thousands of fans visit Graceland each year, making a journey to the home of the King. The amazing number of people who visit his home and buy his memorabilia and recordings is evidence of his continuing popularity. Thousands camped out at Graceland to buy the commemorative Elvis stamp on the day it was first sold, while post offices across the country were mobbed the day the stamp went on sale.

Elvis's legacy cannot be measured. He was the inspiration for a whole generation of rock performers and songwriters. Without Elvis, we might never have heard of Carl Perkins, Jerry Lee Lewis, Johnny Cash, Roy Orbison, the Beatles, or the Rolling Stones. White America might never have discovered the incredible richness of southern black music. He was the wellspring for the whole rock revolution.

Of all the thousands of performing artists who attempt a career, hundreds may achieve success, many may achieve celebrity, and a very few may become superstars. One has achieved artistic immortality: That one is the King.

"You have to put on a show to draw a crowd. If I just stood up there and sang and never moved, people would say, 'I could stay home and listen to his records.' You have to give them a show, something to talk about."

ELVIS

Some No. 1 Singles

"All Shook Up"

"Heartbreak Hotel"

"Don't Be Cruel"

"Love Me Tender"

"Teddy Bear"

"Are You Lonesome Tonight?"

"Jailhouse Rock"

"It's Now or Never"

"Stuck on You"

"A Big Hunk o' Love"

"Good Luck Charm"

"Surrender"

The Basic Elvis Recording Library

The Complete Sun Sessions

Elvis Aron Presley

Elvis's Christmas Album

Elvis's Golden Records

Essential Elvis—The First Movies

A Golden Celebration

The Million Dollar Quartet

Movies and Theater Productions Based on or Inspired by Elvis's Life or Legend

★ *Orpheus Descending* (1957 play by Tennessee Williams, later adapted into a film called *The Fugitive Kind*)

★ *Sing, Boy, Sing* (1958 movie about an Elvis-like singer: Elvis was offered the leading role but turned it down. Tommy Sands played it instead.)

★ *Bye-Bye Birdie* (musical about Elvis-inspired character's being drafted)

E L V I S

* "The Once and Future King" ("Twilight Zone" episode in which an Elvis impersonator accidently kills Elvis)
* *The Living Legend* (1978 Broadway show)
* *Elvis* (1978 TV movie with Kurt Russell)
* *Forever Elvis* (1981 rock musical)
* *Elvis: An American Musical* (1988 theatrical production)
* *Mystery Train* (1989 Jim Jarmusch film)
* *Honeymoon in Vegas* (1992 film in which Nicolas Cage falls in with an Elvis impersonators' convention)
* *This Is Elvis* (David Wolper documentary)

E L V I S

Factoids

✯ When he was a teenager, Elvis bought his clothes at a store called Lansky's, which featured clothes with a lightning logo. Presley took the symbol for his own.

✯ Elvis Presley's great-great-great-grandmother, Morning Dove, was a full-blooded Cherokee Indian.

✯ One of Elvis's first TV appearances was on a program hosted by Steve Allen. He wore a tuxedo and sang "Hound Dog" to a basset hound.

✻ In 1957, Elvis recorded "Teddy Bear" and told the press that he loved teddy bears and never traveled without one. After that, fans sent him hundreds of bears.

✻ Elvis Presley's serial number in the army was 533-1076-1.

✻ Elvis's favorite sport was football. Another favorite was karate. He did his own karate stunts in the movie *G.I. Blues*.

✻ In 1965, the Beatles met Elvis. They were so tongue-tied at meeting the legend that they could only stare dumbly at him until he broke the ice.

✦The Soviet Union sent flowers to Elvis's funeral.

✦Priscilla Beaulieu Presley has become a talented entertainment personality in her own right since her divorce from Elvis. Among her credits are roles in the popular prime-time TV serial "Dallas" and the hit motion pictures *The Naked Gun* and *The Naked Gun 2 1/2*, as well as co-host of a TV show called "Those Amazing Animals."

✦Graceland sells *The Presley Family Cookbook*, which features some of Elvis's favorite recipes.

E L V I S

★ Barbra Streisand's first choice for the lead role in the remake of *A Star Is Born* was Elvis Presley.

★ The first Elvis stamp was issued in Grenada in 1979. Other countries to issue Elvis stamps were Germany, Dominica, and Madagascar.

★ In 1993, the United States Postal Service issued an Elvis stamp. The Postal Service sponsored a contest so that U.S. citizens could vote on which image they wanted: Elvis as a young man or as he looked just before he died. The younger Elvis image won.

The text of this book is set in Matrix,
with Rundfunk and Ribbon display.

Book design by Maura Fadden Rosenthal